B.A.S.I.L.D.O.N.

Workbook to generate and store ideas

Your name:

Starting date:

www.spanishthinkingcoach.com

Introduction

When I was studying at the Open University I used to read, underline and make comments in the books while I was commuting. On many occasions I wanted to write about my own thoughts and ideas. Always I carried a notebook in my bag and I used to write things, such as my plans for the week or any topic and thoughts I was interested about. That is how I wrote my books "Essex Creativity", "Creatividad Vasca" and "Creative Thinking for Londoners".

I continue with the habit of writing in my notebook. When I wrote "Essex Creativity", the first acronym I designed was named "B.A.S.I.L.D.O.N." and consists of groups of different type of techniques to generate ideas. It is easy to remember it in the following way:

Brainstorming   Analogies
Searching   Inspiration
Lottery   Differences
Open questions   Notebook

They are different type of group of techniques. At the same time, each of them can be done in many different ways. For example, if we think about Brainstorming, the traditional way of doing it is in a group of people, without criticising, encouraging quantity as anything can be useful to suggest other type of ideas, in a fast pace. However, it could be done individually, by just writing a list of ideas in a non-judgemental attitude, trying to pour ideas that later will be analysed. In a group, it could also be done by individuals writing ideas in individual papers that are passed onto other members of the group to read them and add other ideas. With today´s technology, social media can be used in such a way that instant messages, chatting, email, blogging, etc. can be used to generate ideas.

When I am commuting by train, I always carry a notebook that I can use to write things while I am in the train. Sometimes I could prefer to read the newspaper or to sleep (looking for inspiration...), but most of the times I am writing ideas in my notebook, not necessarily following the tools I am mentioning above. Sometimes, I feel a bit embarrassed thinking about what other people might think about me as I am aware that I can be very passionate and write at speed when ideas with emotions are flowing out of my mind through the pen into the notebook. Most of the times there are people sleeping, reading the newspaper or checking information (or playing) on their mobile phones.

There are two thoughts that come to my mind: On one side I am very pleased to be able to enjoy this time of the day, especially when magic things happen (ideas that I write that even surprise myself). On the other side, I feel that there is a lot of time wasted, as people might commute 5 days a week, maybe for more than one hour (I assume that when coming back from work people may be tired to think), and these 5 hours could be a wonderful opportunity to enjoy feeling the creativity that flow from you and thinking about good things to do in your life, what is very inspiring. In my case, when commuting, I write things in the notebook, and during the weekend or during my rest days, I tend to transform the idea into something real. For example, the idea for this workbook came while using a notebook to apply B.A.S.I.L.D.O.N. to the question of "How to create more information products for my business idea".

Then, the idea of this notebook is to have a toolbox of techniques to generate ideas that are simple to use and that can be stored to keep them organised in some way till the moment you decide to implement them. I have many times written ideas in many notebooks, and when I am ready to implement them, I cannot find them.

So, this workbook has an index where you can write the topic you are thinking about and you will see the page number, so you can retrieve it easily, or retrieve them easily if you have thought on several occasions about similar topics, for example: career change, job promotion, innovations at work, or other type of ideas for personal enjoyment such as holidays, surprises to give to somebody, poems, letters, activities, etc.
In my website you will find many different ways of using these tools. For this workbook I am going to summarise an easy, fast and entertaining way of using them (you can spend more time and do more things if you wish).

Brainstorming

Just write a list of, for example, 20 ideas about the topic you are thinking about. When thinking about how to improve my business, one of the ideas was to create more products, doing them in simple but useful way.

Analogies

Write two columns. In the first column, write under one concept, a list of things that are related to it and in the next column write under the topic of your thinking, the analogies/suggestions that each of the concepts provoke. In my case I wrote:

Diamond	My business idea
Brilliant	Enthusiastic
Hard	Optimistic, hopeful
Precious	Ideas to resolve problems in society such as unemployment or desmotivation.
Etc. etc.	

There are no right or wrong answers. This is just a way to provoke new ideas.

Searching

Here I write what information I could find and where. For example, thinking about social enterprises, I thought I should explore my local council, networking events and big social enterprises that at the same type support other social enterprises.

Or maybe, which websites I could check to find information, such as libraries, websites for start-ups, etc. Usually I am with my mobile, so even if it is a bit slow, I also can use my mobile to do some searches. You could write what words to put in the search box when going home (to look in a search engine of websites, blogs, presentations, videos, images, etc.).

Inspiration
This relates to the ideas that can come while you are doing something else like having a bath, sleeping or walking around. Even when looking at different type of magazines or books in a library or bookshop. Keep the notebook close to your bed so you can add ideas at any time.

Lottery
In this case I just look for a random word to look for suggestions for the ideas I am looking for. When I was commuting in the train, there was this announcement about the next stop and when I looked I saw the word XXX Street, so I thought about links to the word "street".

The good thing about this technique is that forces you to look into different ideas. In my case, I thought that as a social enterprise trying to promote creative thinking among teenagers, maybe I could ask permission to the council to put some type of posters or sculptures that can remind people to think innovatively and how to make decisions. The posters could be displayed also around schools.

Differences
When thinking about different products that can help to promote creative thinking, I thought about books, workbooks, videos, ebooks, websites, etc. and when thinking about changes, I thought about the possibility of writing songs.

I am not very good at music, but I know that there are some well-known songs that are on the public domain, so I could use this music and create my own lyrics (words) related to the topic of creativity and personal development.

Usually when thinking about differences, I think about changes. For example, when thinking about a book, you could think about size (small, medium, large), format (paperback or electronic), type of distribution (from my website, from on demand publishers, from books shops, etc.), about the level (beginner, medium, advanced), etc. Also you could think about the steps in a process (service) and how each step could be changed in some way.

Open Questions
Asking questions is the basics for creative thinking. When you ask yourself a question, you are giving yourself an opportunity to think and the more questions, the more answers.

In my case, I asked myself a list of questions and when thinking about to increase my income, I asked myself:

Which new products could I design and produce in little time?

The answers to this question lead me to think about new products that use my previous ideas but covering other type of needs.

Notebook
This is just to write about your topic, as when writing about your topic of thought there are more ideas that flow automatically. It is like when somebody is listening to you. When you are talking about the topic, at the same time you are thinking about it.

I usually follow the acronym I designed for my book "Essex Creativity" called W.A.I.T. (Write, A for underline, Interrogate, Try to answer) in which I <u>w</u>rite about the topic (one or two pages), later I (<u>A</u>) underline things that I feel are interesting, then I ask questions (<u>I</u>nterrogate) related to what I have underlined and finally I <u>t</u>ry to answer them (with my own thoughts or searching information in books, internet, etc.).

In my case, when I was writing about my business idea, I underlined something about asking for advice in the library or the council and then this lead me to ask myself who else could help me and then I wrote a list of other people who could help me.

If you prefer, you can use this area of "Notebook" to draw something about it.

As mentioned before, this is a workbook to promote thinking and to store your ideas, so the index will show the pages where each session starts and then you can write the topic you want to get ideas for. I have not indicated tools to express the ideas, so feel free to use pens of different colours to or markers to highlight ideas that you find the most useful ones. Also you can use this workbook to re-read your ideas in the future and add new ones.

Index	Topics	Page

1. Ideas for: _____

BRAINSTORMING

ANALOGIES

_____   _____

SEARCHING

INSPIRATION

LOTTERY

DIFFERENCES

OPEN QUESTIONS

NOTEBOOK

Here you can continue with NOTEBOOK and/or write which are the most important ideas/thoughts for you.

2. Ideas for: _____

BRAINSTORMING

ANALOGIES

_____   _____

SEARCHING

INSPIRATION

LOTTERY

DIFFERENCES

OPEN QUESTIONS

NOTEBOOK

Here you can continue with NOTEBOOK and/or write which are the most important ideas/thoughts for you.

3. Ideas for: _____

BRAINSTORMING

ANALOGIES

_____   _____

SEARCHING

INSPIRATION

LOTTERY

DIFFERENCES

OPEN QUESTIONS

NOTEBOOK

Here you can continue with NOTEBOOK and/or write which are the most important ideas/thoughts for you.

4. Ideas for: _____

BRAINSTORMING

ANALOGIES

_____   _____

SEARCHING

INSPIRATION

LOTTERY

DIFFERENCES

OPEN QUESTIONS

NOTEBOOK

Here you can continue with NOTEBOOK and/or write which are the most important ideas/thoughts for you.

5. Ideas for: _____

BRAINSTORMING

ANALOGIES

_____   _____

SEARCHING

INSPIRATION

LOTTERY

DIFFERENCES

OPEN QUESTIONS

NOTEBOOK

Here you can continue with NOTEBOOK and/or write which are the most important ideas/thoughts for you.

6. Ideas for: _____

BRAINSTORMING

ANALOGIES

_____   _____

SEARCHING

INSPIRATION

LOTTERY

DIFFERENCES

OPEN QUESTIONS

NOTEBOOK

Here you can continue with NOTEBOOK and/or write which are the most important ideas/thoughts for you.

7. Ideas for: _____

BRAINSTORMING

ANALOGIES

_____   _____

SEARCHING

INSPIRATION

LOTTERY

DIFFERENCES

OPEN QUESTIONS

NOTEBOOK

Here you can continue with NOTEBOOK and/or write which
are the most important ideas/thoughts for you.

8. Ideas for: _____

BRAINSTORMING

ANALOGIES

_____   _____

SEARCHING

INSPIRATION

LOTTERY

DIFFERENCES

OPEN QUESTIONS

NOTEBOOK

Here you can continue with NOTEBOOK and/or write which are the most important ideas/thoughts for you.

9. Ideas for: _____

BRAINSTORMING

ANALOGIES

_____   _____

SEARCHING

INSPIRATION

LOTTERY

DIFFERENCES

OPEN QUESTIONS

NOTEBOOK

Here you can continue with NOTEBOOK and/or write which are the most important ideas/thoughts for you.

10. Ideas for: _____

BRAINSTORMING

ANALOGIES

_____   _____

SEARCHING

INSPIRATION

LOTTERY

DIFFERENCES

OPEN QUESTIONS

NOTEBOOK

Here you can continue with NOTEBOOK and/or write which are the most important ideas/thoughts for you.

11. Ideas for: _____

BRAINSTORMING

ANALOGIES

_____   _____

SEARCHING

INSPIRATION

LOTTERY

DIFFERENCES

OPEN QUESTIONS

NOTEBOOK

Here you can continue with NOTEBOOK and/or write which are the most important ideas/thoughts for you.

12. Ideas for: _____

BRAINSTORMING

ANALOGIES

_____   _____

SEARCHING

INSPIRATION

LOTTERY

DIFFERENCES

OPEN QUESTIONS

NOTEBOOK

Here you can continue with NOTEBOOK and/or write which are the most important ideas/thoughts for you.

13. Ideas for: _____

BRAINSTORMING

ANALOGIES

_____   _____

SEARCHING

INSPIRATION

LOTTERY

DIFFERENCES

OPEN QUESTIONS

NOTEBOOK

Here you can continue with NOTEBOOK and/or write which are the most important ideas/thoughts for you.

14. Ideas for: _____

BRAINSTORMING

ANALOGIES

_____   _____

SEARCHING

INSPIRATION

LOTTERY

DIFFERENCES

OPEN QUESTIONS

NOTEBOOK

Here you can continue with NOTEBOOK and/or write which are the most important ideas/thoughts for you.

15. Ideas for: _____

BRAINSTORMING

ANALOGIES

_____   _____

SEARCHING

INSPIRATION

LOTTERY

DIFFERENCES

OPEN QUESTIONS

NOTEBOOK

Here you can continue with NOTEBOOK and/or write which are the most important ideas/thoughts for you.

16. Ideas for: _____

BRAINSTORMING

ANALOGIES

_____   _____

SEARCHING

INSPIRATION

LOTTERY

DIFFERENCES

OPEN QUESTIONS

NOTEBOOK

Here you can continue with NOTEBOOK and/or write which are the most important ideas/thoughts for you.

17. Ideas for: _____

BRAINSTORMING

ANALOGIES

_____   _____

SEARCHING

.

.

INSPIRATION

LOTTERY

DIFFERENCES

OPEN QUESTIONS

NOTEBOOK

Here you can continue with NOTEBOOK and/or write which are the most important ideas/thoughts for you.

18. Ideas for: _____

BRAINSTORMING

ANALOGIES

_____   _____

SEARCHING

INSPIRATION

LOTTERY

DIFFERENCES

OPEN QUESTIONS

NOTEBOOK

Here you can continue with NOTEBOOK and/or write which are the most important ideas/thoughts for you.

19. Ideas for: _____

BRAINSTORMING

ANALOGIES

_____   _____

SEARCHING

INSPIRATION

LOTTERY

DIFFERENCES

OPEN QUESTIONS

NOTEBOOK

Here you can continue with NOTEBOOK and/or write which are the most important ideas/thoughts for you.

20. Ideas for: _____

BRAINSTORMING

ANALOGIES

_____   _____

SEARCHING

INSPIRATION

LOTTERY

DIFFERENCES

OPEN QUESTIONS

NOTEBOOK

Here you can continue with NOTEBOOK and/or write which are the most important ideas/thoughts for you.

Which have been the most useful ideas and why?

Other books written by Miguel Acha:

- Essex Creativity
- Creative Thinking for Londoners
- Young Inventors Workbook

These books and many other resources can be found in my website:

www.spanishthinkingcoach.com